POEMS ALONG THE WAY

Alexandra Mason

"I Walk the Arduous Road" appears on
Oregon Poetic Voices

1st edition published as Sandra Mason
2nd edition ©Alexandra Mason, 2017
ISBN-13:978-0692875360
ISBN-10:0692875360
Turnstone Books of Oregon, LLC
Seal Rock, OR

For Donny King,
my partner along the way

CONTENTS

FOREWORD

"A Retired Scholar at the Lotus Pool," who edited an eighteenth-century collection of *Three Hundred T'ang Poems*, based his title on this Chinese saying:

"By reading thoroughly three hundred T'ang poems, one will write verse without learning."

As a poet, I have found these artifacts of a millennium and a half ago spellbinding and ageless. Drawing inspiration from their poetic moment, I have endeavored to enter the spirit of the conversation by reworking several of the poems from a contemporary perspective, striving to maintain what Kenneth Rexroth has called their "immediacy of utterance" and William Carlos Williams their "subtlety of lyrical candor."

Western readers have for decades enjoyed Witter Bynner's translation with Kiang Kang-Hu of the three hundred, first published in 1929 as *The Jade Mountain* and reprinted consistently in 1931, 1945, 1951, 1957, 1964, and 1972. In his introduction to the volume, Bynner mentions the impossibility of definitive translation. As there will be variable interpretations of a poem written in English, so there will axiomatically be for poems in other languages. With Chinese, which lacks verb tenses, personal pronouns, and words of logical connection, a western reader participates perhaps even more fully in constructing the poetic meaning For Bynner, then, even his "translations" were interpretive versions of the originals.

C. H. Kwock and Vincent McHugh in "A Translator's Dialogue" at the end of their book *Old Friend From Far Away* (1980) locate the truth of translation of poetry from Chinese to English. Considering the advice of Stanley Burnshaw to translate precisely word for word or violate the original, they conclude, "It's possible . . . to translate a poem word for word with the most desperate fidelity and *not only not get* that *poem but get no poem at all*." Because of the condensation of Chinese grammar and notation, faithful translation is truly impossible, a feat compounded by the nature of poetry itself. As Holmes Welch notes in *Taoism: The Parting of the Way* (1957, 1965), "with most of Chinese poetry and with much of Chinese prose, we have to decide for ourselves what is meant, within more or less broad limits set by the text. To read is an act of creation." I have striven throughout to be both respectful and creative, to preserve each poet's "own way to magic," as Lu Chi says, but also to observe a tight structure that will "trap heaven and earth in the cage of form."

My method has been to work from literal translation of each Chinese character. When these words are strung together sequentially, I begin to find structure and progression in the sense of the lines, their images and metaphors, their ironies and turns. I then read several other translations of the poem and put everything aside for awhile, coming back to the poem later with a blended notion of meaning. As I work through the poem line by line, I find that at some moment the poem's intention appears to me clearly. If a context seems too obscure to work in English, I seek an equivalent, bringing in no doubt resonances from both British and American traditions. Here is an example of how I move through a poem from the transliteration. This is the final poem of the collection:

RETURNING HOME (after He Zhizhang)	CIRCLE VILLAGE IMAGE BOOK / LETTER (He Zhizhang)
As a young boy, I left my town; now, an oldster, I circle home. The place seems as it was; yet I have changed, my mane of hair now but a shabby pelt. Here comes a grandson, image of myself. He smiles politely and inquires, *Stranger, where is your home?*	YOUNG SMALL DEPART -IAN [ONE WHO] OLD ELDEST RETURN VILLAGE NEWS NO ALTER HAIR ON TEMPLES FUR FEEBLE SON BOY MUTUAL MEET NOT IMAGE TO KNOW SMILE TO ASK VISITOR FROM WHAT PLACE TO COME

What results, then, is a reworking of the original, following William Carlos Williams's observation that "Without a new language into which the poems could be rendered their meaning would have been lost." Readers have found these new versions calming, philosophical, and moving. My intent has been both composition and homage. With Witter Bynner I believe that my versions "accent in these T'ang masterpieces the human and universal qualities by which they have endured."

Many other poets — Ezra Pound, Arthur Waley, Amy Lowell, Burton Watson, Red Pine, David Young, Kenneth Rexroth, Gary Snyder, William Carlos Williams, and David Hinton, for example — have followed Bynner in reworking a few or several of the masterpieces. A reader who examines many English versions of the same original will realize that even these ostensibly same poems carry divergent movements and nuance. A translator chooses what to elide and what to expand on logically. A translator envisions the "place" of the poem and gives it body. One of Li Bai's most famous poems is generally titled "Drinking Alone with the Moon."

The poem's final line, based on the transliteration

"each other / time period / remote / cloud / Chinese or Han Dynasty,"

is rendered variously as:

"For you my boon companions dear
Come only when the sky is clear,"

"The next time that we meet shall be
 Beside yon distant milky way,"

"May we long share our odd, inanimate feast,
And meet at last on the Cloudy River of the sky,"

"And often hail each other at evening
 Far across the vast and vaporous space!"

"We three
forever-silent friends
will meet some day
in the clouds up above,"

"Thus we'll pursue our own avatars,
And we'll all meet again in the River of
Staaaaaaars!"

"may we meet again someday
 in the white river of stars
 overhead!"

and

"Promise me we'll be friends for ever,
do this again with the stars in heaven."

We can see that the poems follow the same general
narrative pattern but that their word choices,
poetic styles, and phrasing open up sometimes

remarkably different nuances. You may enjoy looking at examples of this poem from various decades of the past hundred years:

I.   **On Drinking Alone by Moonlight**
        Trans. Ezra Pound, 1915

Here are flowers and here is wine,
But where's a friend with me to join
Hand in hand and heart to heart
In one full cup before we part?

Rather than to drink alone,
I'll make bold to ask the moon
To condescend to lend her face
The hour and the scene to grace.

Lo, she answers, and she brings
My shadow on her silver wings;
That makes three, and we shall be.
I ween, a merry company

The modest moon declines the cup,
But shadow promptly takes it up,
And when I dance my shadow fleet
Keeps measure with my flying feet.

But though the moon declines to tipple
She dances in yon shining ripple,
And when I sing, my festive song,
The echoes of the moon prolong.

Say, when shall we next meet together?
Surely not in cloudy weather,

For you my boon companions dear
Come only when the sky is clear.

II.   We Three
Trans. Arthur Waley, 1919

One pot of wine amid the Flowers
Alone I pour, and none with me.
The cup I lift; the Moon invite;
Who with my shadow makes us three.
The moon then drinks without a pause.
The shadow does what I begin.
The shadow, Moon and I in free
Rejoice until the spring come in.
I sing: and wavers time the moon.
I dance: the shadow antics too.
Our joys we share while sober still.
When drunk, we part and bid adieu.
Of loveless outing this the pact,
Which we all swear to keep for aye.
The next time that we meet shall be
Beside yon distant milky way.

III.   Drinking Alone by Moonlight
Trans. Florence Ayscough & Amy Lowell, 1921

A cup of wine, under the flowering trees;
I drink alone, for no friend is near.
Raising my cup I beckon the bright moon,
For he, with my shadow, will make three men.
The moon, alas, is no drinker of wine;

Listless, my shadow creeps about at my side.
Yet with the moon as friend and the shadow
as slave
I must make merry before the Spring is spent.
To the songs I sing the moon flickers her
beams;
In the dance I weave my shadow tangles and
breaks.
While we were sober, three shared the fun;
Now we are drunk, each goes his way.
May we long share our odd, inanimate feast,
And meet at last on the Cloudy River of the
sky.

IV.   **Three with the Moon and his Shadow**
        Trans. Witter Bynner, 1929

With a jar of wine I sit by the flowering trees.
I drink alone, and where are my friends?
Ah, the moon above looks down on me;
I call and lift my cup to his brightness.
And see, there goes my shadow before me.
Ho! We're a party of three, I say,–
Though the poor moon can't drink,
And my shadow but dances around me,
We're all friends to-night,
The drinker, the moon and the shadow.
Let our revelry be suited to the spring!

I sing, the wild moon wanders the sky.
I dance, my shadow goes tumbling about.
While we're awake, let us join in carousal;
Only sweet drunkenness shall ever part us.

Let us pledge a friendship no mortals know,
And often hail each other at evening
Far across the vast and vaporous space.

V.   Under the Moon: Drinking Alone
       *Trans. C. H. Kwock and Vincent McHugh,
       1958*

per amica silentia lunae

Flowers all round
        One pot of wine
Solitary
        drinking without a friend
I raise my cup
        to invite
        the bright moon
With my shadow
        We make three:
the moon
        --though it doesn't know how to dance
and my shadow
        --which can only follow me
For the moment
        I'll make do
        With moon and shadow
Enjoyment
        Is fitting
        to the spring

I sing
    and the moon
    wavers to and fro
I dance
    and my shadow
    gets all mixed up
Sober
    we frolic together
Drunk
    each goes his way alone
We three
    forever-silent friends
will meet some day
    In the clouds up above

VI.   Drinking Alone Under the Moon
Trans. Burton Watson, 1986

Among the flowers, with a flask of wine,
I drink all alone–no one to share.
Raising my flask, I welcome the moon,
And my shadow joins us, making a
threesome.

As I sing, the moon seems to sway back and
forth;
As I dance, my shadow goes flopping about.
As long as we're sober, we'll enjoy one
another,
And when we get drunk, we'll go our own
ways.

[x]

Thus we'll pursue our own avatars,
And we'll all meet again in the River of
Staaaaaaars!

VII.   **Drinking in Moonlight**
Trans. David Young, 1990

I sit with my wine jar
among flowers
blossoming trees

no one to drink with

well, there's the moon

I raise my cup
and ask him to join me
bringing my shadow
making us three

but the moon doesn't seem to be drinking
and my shadow just creeps around behind me

still, we're companions tonight
me, the moon, and the shadow
we're observing
the rites of spring

I sing
and the moon rocks back and forth
I dance

and my shadow
weaves and tumbles with me

we celebrate for awhile
then go our own ways, drunk
may we meet again someday
in the white river of stars
overhead!

VIII.   Off His Face in the Flower Border
Trans. Steven D. Owyoung, 2011

Sitting in the flowers with a bottle of wine,
alone, I pour another glass
and raise it to salute the moon,
who, with my shadow, makes three of us.

The moon's not drinking;
my shadow's a copycat;
let's have fun anyway,
enjoy Spring while we can.

I sing: the moon dances.
I dance: my shadow staggers.
While I drink, they're my best friends:
when I fall over, they scatter.

Promise me we'll be friends for ever,
do this again with the stars in heaven.

My version:

Drinking alone with the Moon (after Li Bai)
Alexandra Mason, 2012

Alone, as the moon begins its descent,
I pour a cup of wine.
Like a single pansy in a pot, lonely,
I pour the wine.
With no friends near,
I raise a congenial toast,
inviting the bright moon to join me.
My shadow, the moon, and I — a joyful trio.
The faltering moon's done imbibing,
and my shadow apes me like a disciple —
I must drink for us all.
I sing a song to lighten
our way along the road —
a song to welcome spring.
The moon keeps its falling course
as I sing a serenade
and dance, forth and back,
my shadow unconfused.
Together we awaken the season;
together we are joyous.
We feel the wine's headiness
and collapse, isolate again.
Together, we were content to stay;
separate again, each of us
longs for our home
as distant as the Milky Way.

While I have chosen only fifty-two of the three hundred for this volume, I conceive their narrative order as a spiritual journey, and one may find satisfaction in reading the entire sequence in a single long sitting. Many voices tell the story with clear and distinctive humanity of perception, thought, emotion. I have tried to capture these distinctive voices. Yet I have chosen fifty-two poems purposely so that the volume may also be a stimulus for weekly meditation throughout the duration of a year.

The poems are suitable for meditation because to my mind they are Taoist in apprehension and outlook. Many of these poets served as governmental officials and traveled as part of their position. Some fell out politically and were sent into exile. The journey, traveling through life as if on a path, was both actuality and metaphor to them. As Deng Ming-Dao has reminded me, the Tao is represented in Chinese characters as "a person on a path."

(Calligraphy by Jian-ye Jiang)

Each poem is a portion of the journey, and the narrative sequence outlines an emotional philosophical process of life's journey along the way. All felt the natural world as an integral part of life. They had also experienced the vicissitudes of uncertainty in the world, which gave them an often ironic perspective that appears as a thrilling turn in the poems.

The poems chronicle travel and return; solitude and sociability; kinship and isolation; desire and void. They often contain a Keatsian moment of "negative capability," of identification with something animate or inanimate in nature—a cicada, a goose, the moon—wherein the poet projects into the emotive life of the "other."

No doubt this project came to me as a natural progression of my own poetic and philosophical experience, first, as a scholar of Shakespeare and of poetry in English, and second, as a sojourner from mid-life on the paths of t'ai chi and of the Tao. These poems have an immediacy that has calmed my own spirit and, as the adage predicts, made me a better poet.

独立

QUESTION AND ANSWER ON THE MOUNTAIN
(after Li Bai)

If you ask
why I live
on the green mountain,
I will only smile in reply.
Here my innermost heart
centers itself in indolence.
I watch peach blossoms
float to far downstream.
Alone I find heaven on earth
apart from the world of man.

I WALK THE ARDUOUS ROAD
(after Li Bai)

I.

Before me
a bottle of China's best wine
and dainty treats in a jade dish
worth a king's coffer.
My appetite shriveled,
I overturn the cup,
toss away my chopsticks.
I startle and pull my sword,
my eyes scanning
north west south and east
yet I know not what I seek
or what to fear.
I would ferry over the river,
clogged with ice,
climb the highest peak with vim
yet snow palls under a gloomy sky.
I sit and idly dangle bait
into the blue creek,
dreaming again of chasing the sun
as it dips into the sea.

How hard seems my path,
how inscrutable my destiny.
Byways tempt me with indecision.
Be calm and simply trust!
As wind circling the globe
settles the sea,
I will hoist my sail like a cloud
and set out toward the measureless unknown.

II.

The way stretches before me
broad as the blue-green heavens.
Alone, I feel uneasy,
abashed to walk in the still footprints of sages,
ashamed to journey with the throng,
who squander their time
wagering on cockfights
for a trifle.
Some ply their sword
as if it were a lute,
their song a sad memorial to war.
Others bow uneasily to tyrants,
muddy the clear river with trade,
supplant the true magistrate
with greed and graft.
We do not know our king—
in olden days—remember?—he celebrated artists,
parading them along the top of lofty city walls.
On festival day he walked amid the crowd
clearing the way, sweeping with a stick broom.

3

He played a humble role
in the drama of state,
inspiring us to kindness and to peace.
Today our livers are weak,
our hearts cowardly.
Soldiers palely mime brave heroes
of lore.
Now our garden goes to weed;
wild turnip stems wind 'round white bones
of our illustrious king.
We work only for yellow gelt.
The way is hard.
How shall I tread?
And how will I find my home?

III.

No wise man washes out his ear
with the river at full flood
or stuffs his mouth
with bracken grown in full sun.
Tiring in a confused world
to let the soul's ray gleam.
Why choose the lonely way,
aiming higher than the clouds
and moon? In the mirror,
behold, an old man, dignified,
accomplishments his crown.
Surely such worth
outlasts its fragile vessel.
At midnight I dream of the great souls

sailing the river of heaven.
They toss me a rope,
a line to the safe shore
free from the scorn of earthly men.
Even there
how can I keep my heart secure,
defend my way?
No one's exempt from life's travail
nor can we choose our death.
The tax man exacts
his due upon his date.
Yet tonight in this pavilion
how glorious the cry of the crane!
Ancestors confidently trod the path
toting their dark falcon.
Today our heroes have vanished.
We cling to workaday lives
but with the harvest recall
our journey west which beckons.
This cup of wine before me
makes me giddy.
Need I seek fame,
my name to last
a thousand years?

THE GOLDEN ROBE:
ADVICE TO A YOUNG MAN
(after Du Qiuniang)

Do not seek to wear the gilded robe;
swaddle yourself in golden days of youth.

Pluck the rose the moment that it blooms —
or, old and gray, you'll gather only stems.

IN SPRING
(after Li Bai)

Here the grass is stained
the green of jade silk.
As the mulberry branch droops,
monarch of myself, I dream of home.
As another's thrall
I am heartsick, day by day.
Others, not I, can know
the song of spring, the ways of love.
Yet right now what hand
parts the gauze curtain
that surrounds my bed?

防雨

CROWS CALLING AT NIGHT
(after Li Bai)

Under a yellow cloud
the crow rests
beside a wall near the tower.
With a call of caw-caw,
up he flies, returning
to his branch.
The Qin River girl
plies her loom,
weaving a fine brocade.
The tapestry's green yarn
frames her as if in a window,
and I see her as through a mist.
She does not speak, and
her shuttle too falls silent.
Memory revives
the discontent of love,
her man now far away.
Alone within her solitary room
she hides
and her tears
bring the rain.

A LIFE LAMENT
(after Wang Changling)

Unsure, she sweeps the hall
of the Golden Palace
with her round fan,
back and forth.
Her pale face
will darken only
with the shadow
of the crow.

眼泪湿

BITTER LOVE
(after Li Bai)

Again tonight the maiden
rolls up the beaded curtain
of her window.
I see her furrowed brow,
her face lined with sorrow.
Wet tears still corrode
her cheeks.
Does her heart yet know
its foe?

女人的脸

AUTUMN AIR
(after Li Bai)

The autumn wind seems as lucid
as the moon is bright.
It gathers the fallen leaves
then suddenly scatters them,
startling the jackdaw from his perch.
My friend, you show the world
your daytime face
but now, tonight,
suffer the untold pain.

HEARING A FLUTE ON A SPRING NIGHT
(after Li Bai)

I hear a jade flute,
a secret sound flying
through the city.
I seek the house
where a lone soul plays,
yet as spring wind
fills the streets with whispers,
I lose direction.
Hearing such a nocturne,
so heavy with sadness
it could snap a willow branch,
who would not long
to return home?

精神痛苦

LONG YEARNING
(after Li Bai)

For years here in Chang'an
my soul has ached.
Tonight the dog bays
a welcome to autumn;
moon shadows encage me
in a golden web.
My heart is sequestered
as in a walled well
covered with hoar-frost.
My bamboo mat gleams like ice.
As the lamp loses its will
and sputters, I pull back the curtain,
gazing at the lonely moon.
My long sigh escapes, yet in vain,
for my flower-love lives
at the far end of another cloud.
Above us, a black sky looms,
the highest heaven;
below us, green waters billow.
The road to heaven is slow
for the bitter spirit

(continued)

longing to fly from no-man's land.
Even in dreams my spirit is stymied,
the mountain pass impenetrable.
My soul aches.

GAZING INTO SPACE
(after Du Fu)

Toward the west snow shrouds the mountain
and the three walled cities with frost.
To the south the beach gleams clear,
flanking the river's long bridge.
I am a sea of emptiness
swept by dusty winds,
longing for my brothers.
The infinite horizon echoes my solitude
and I must weep.
Alone I face the sunset of my life
sure to be beset with disease.
I'm like dust in the corner of a vast hall
of the imperial court.
I mount my horse to journey
into the void,
my eye on the edge of the world.
How can men endure this world
of perpetual sadness?

THE LONG ASCENT
(after Du Fu)

Even apes hiss
as wind hurries through the sky.
On the river isle the snowy egret
returns to its sandy nest.
Leaves fall mournfully,
no edge between tree and ground.
The river rolls on, a long, eternal flow.
Its ten thousand miles of sadness
bring autumn to all who live.
I feel ancient, infirm,
climbing alone to the mountain shrine.
Each of my frosty hairs
tallies my pain and distress.
The rains pour down again
and my wine transforms to mud.

想法

THOUGHTS
(after Zhang Jiuling)

A lone bean goose skims the sea,
shunning the lesser ponds.
On shore he spies two small green birds
nesting in the three-pearl tree.
With your treasure in the tree-top
do you not fear golden bullets?
The envious slander those
with beautiful attire.
The tall rise up
toward heaven in their scorn.

Today the path I roam is dark and deep.
Assassin, do you wait in ambush here?

梦想

THINKING OF AN EXILED FRIEND
(after Zhang Jiuling)

As the moon grows bright above the sea tonight
water and sky appear as one.
Longing, I see you with my mind's eye
far, far away, in darkness, missing me.
I douse my candle yet
the room is bathed in light.
My clothes are strewn about, my body bare,
yet yearning mutes my chill.
Happily I seek my bed
hoping to dream you near.

指南

TO MY TEACHER
(after Du Fu)

As wind shakes leaves from the trees,
my heart knows the poet's grief.
His words, elegant thoughts,
teach me the way.
Minds span thousands of harvests.
We both sprinkle tears
sharing sadness across time.
His now ruined home nests in a rivered vale,
and only poems endure, written in vain.
Join me in mist on this abandoned terrace —
Was his life a dream?

The ancient palaces all have fallen.
Not even the ferryman
can show you their ruins —
and doubts they truly were.

足跡

THINKING OF MY TAOIST MASTER
(after Wei Yingwu)

This morning, as I feel my study's chill,
my master's name slips quickly into mind.
I see him gathering fuel along the swampy shore,
returning home to heat white stones
to cook his meager soup.
If only I could cheer him with a dram—
to comfort him as leaves flood down
at dusk in wind and storm.
But in the fallen leaves,
could I retrace his steps?

名人堂

TO LI BAI AT THE END OF THE WORLD
(after Du Fu)

Here at the end of the sky
it's a cold wind blows.
I ask that you
resolve for me at midnight
life's small mysteries.

The wild geese fly in autumn
when the waters rise in lakes.

Be wary to achieve a poet's fame.

The mountain elf may charm you
as lifetimes pass away.

Ask the drowning man
if your poems can save him now.

放松

THINKING OF FAME ON A NIGHT JOURNEY
(after Du Fu)

A light wind flutters fine grass
on the shore like sheaves of a book,
shivering the mast at my night mooring.
From a wide-open sky the stars
lean peacefully toward earth
as the moon bubbles up
through the broad river's flow.
How can a poet live by his acclaim?
Agéd, now infirm, I should seek rest.
Yet still I flit from here to there,
as much of note to the universe
as a common gull.

REMINISCENCE FROM A NIGHT-MOORING
(after Li Bai)

From the ox-bank
west of the river tonight
no cloud mars the deep blue sky.
Musing from my boat,
I feel the autumn's approach
and idly recall
the army of General Chi.
Though I chant my verses aloud,
not a warrior lives to hear.
In the morning again
I hoist my sail
as maple leaves
clutter the bank.

花卉展

COALESCENCE
(after Zhang Jiuling)

In spring the orchid is gay and green,
luxuriant with blooms.
In fall the cinnamon flower glows bright.
Both desire to thrive.
They seek their fullest fate.
The forest hermit is content
with news he sniffs in the wind.
The grass and trees are true unto themselves.
Why should I then be tempted from my path?

降序

DESCENDING THE MOUNTAIN
TO A LODGE FOR A DRINK
(after Li Bai)

With the sunset, unhurried,
I descend the mountain,
the rising moon at my back.
The path ahead
disappears in blue shadows,
and I wish for a hand to hold.
Ahead I see the farm house.
Children dart out,
open a thorny gate, beckon
me through the green bamboo
down a hidden path
so narrow the radish greens
brush against my robe.
What joy to have leisure
to rest and talk!
With exquisite wine
we pass the time
and wipe away our cares.

(continued)

We hum a long song loosely,
ending when the stars
dip into the stream.
My host and I are giddy
together, forgetting
all worldly affairs.

朋友

A FAREWELL
(after Li Bai)

Today's sun must make way for tomorrow —
it abandons me with yesterday.
My mind is in disarray, my heart troubled —
we live in a worrisome time.
A distant wind always
brings the wild geese in autumn.
Now I can welcome them only —
drunk — in the courtyard
of a grand manor.
We both have plied our brushes
like the old masters, I emulating you.
We lean on our walking sticks, a sure sign
the book of life nears its close,
your story excelling mine.

Both of us have sought
to transcend the heights
to view the moon from above.
We have sliced the water
with our words
but worries succeed worries

(continued)

as both of us grow old.
With my hair in disarray
I shall steer
a small boat
chasing your image.

SEEING OFF A FRIEND
(after Li Bai)

At the spot where
you can see green hills
beyond the north city wall
and where the rapids
flow east through town,
this is the place to take leave,
and we must part.
The lone tumbleweed
may wander ten thousand miles
as thoughts drift through
a traveler's mind like clouds.
I watch you head toward sunset,
wave a sad hand,
and last I hear your horse
whinny good-bye.

A FAREWELL TO
POET MENG HAO RAN
(after Li Bai)

Good-bye to the west! We embrace
at the Yellow Crane Tower.
As willows blossom to smoke
in spring, you leave for the city of poets.
I see the shadow of a distant single sail
on the verge of the horizon —
only that, and the river flowing to the sky.

GRASSES, OR A POEM
UPON LEAVE-TAKING
(after Bai Juyi)

This season finds the summer's grasses
parched and sere.
Each year the field fires burn
but cannot sap this glory —
like leaves within a book
that flutter open
grass will breathe again
with the fragrant spring wind.
The wind will carry me along the old road
to the village yet another time
to offer you this poem
and bid a sad farewell,
old friends too glum to weep.
Yet the plumed cockscomb is luxuriant.
The plumed cockscomb is luxuriant still.

折磨

ENDLESS YEARNING II
(after Li Bai)

By day the flowers have sucked up all the sun,
leaving only a smoky haze.
By night the moon's bright desire
troubles my sleep.
I hear a halting tune,
a harp from the Double Phoenix,
a song that echoes the ache of the moon.
Such a song belongs to the player alone,
each person's sadness his own.
Perhaps memory will send me
the songbird of hope
like an air on the wind.
I imagine an exile
so far from home
the sky seems to him a stranger,
the sun an unwelcome judge.
Mist troubles my eyes—
now tears spring and flow.
Pity me, won't you, and come back,
for there in the mirror of the moon,
behold my own torment.

THE MOON AT THE FORTIFIED PASS
(after Li Bai)

Tonight the bright moon emerges
from behind the mountain
in a vast ocean of blue clouds.
Here at the pass of the jade gate
the wind is always fierce,
quickening on its epic journey
through the steppes.
All of China seems smothered by snow,
an empty white desert.
My road leads up the mountain
to cast prying eyes
on the marine bay beyond.
Enemy forces unseen
still may lurk.
Those who flee their threat,
passing by our ramparts,
gaze with longing eyes
toward home, bitterly ruing
their flight.
Others, in their mansions,
even now
sleep without a care.

VISITING THE TAOIST PRIEST
BUT NOT FINDING HIM
(after Li Bai)

The sound of a barking dog
ripples the water,
its surface layered thick
with peach blossoms
fallen like rain.
Among the trees
deep in the woods
now and then a deer passes.
The river's rush
drowns out the noon bell
as green mist rises beyond
the wild bamboo wall.
Spring departs,
hanging its verdant flag
along the mountain peak.
I find the house empty —
and sadly consider
the tired pines,
two or three
leaning into the wind.

薄暮

WAITING IN VAIN FOR MY TEACHER
(after Meng Haoran)

The sun has set behind the mountains,
and the gullies are dark with shadows.
As the moon rises behind the pines,
the night grows cool.
My ears buzz with the river's rush
and the wind through the trees.
The woodsmen have returned to their homes,
and birds roost properly in their nests.

You promised to meet me here
at your lodge at dusk;
alone, I bide,
playing my lute to the shrubs.

AT THE HOUSE OF THE TAOIST MONK
(after Liu Chang-Chi'ing)

A single path leads
to the house of the Taoist monk:
only traces of footprints
on the strawberry moss,
a snowy cloud resting on the quiet bank,
spring grasses crowding the vacant doorway.
Years of rain have nurtured the mountain pine.
In the stillness an alpine rill
lined by flowers trills to me its truth —
and I forget all words.

TO A SOLITARY WILD GOOSE
(after Cui Tu)

Your flock has maneuvered
its return to home ground —
only you remain to fly alone.
In the evening rain you call to them
then settle slowly on the icy pond,
passing through clouds
that clothe the bank with gloom.
Through the cold mountain pass
you've flown together,
with strength in numbers
eluding hunters' arrows.
Now, flying all alone,
can you help but doubt your way?

AT MY MOUNTAIN RETREAT
(after Wang Wei)

At the midpoint of my life
I find myself upon the proper path.
Here in my mountain home at dusk
in pleasing solitude, how good to know myself! —
to walk until the river blocks my way,
to sit and watch the clouds as they float by.
And if by chance I meet an aging woodsman,
we chat and laugh, forgetting to go home.

花瓣

FALLEN PETALS
(after Li Shangyin)

When the magistrate departs
I see my garden's disorder:
the rays of a remote sun
light a straying path crowded with growth,
and I cannot rally to clear away
the strewn petals with my broom.
My heart would have the garden as before
yet the late spring weighs on my spirit.
Nothing to do but wait
and wet my clothes with tears.

YELLOW CRANE TOWER
(after Cui Hao)

An immortal left here on a yellow crane;
the empty tower honors his ascent.
That single yellow crane has not returned,
and for a thousand years
the sky's been white with sad and empty clouds.
The river clearly mirrors the sun tree
as lush plumed grasses thrive on Parrot Island.
The sun sets in the mountain pass—
how am I to live?
That mist rising over the river
is worrisome.

月球

A SONG OF THE MOON
FOR MY FAMILY AND FRIENDS
IN THESE TROUBLED TIMES
(after Bai Juyi)

These days no joy in books or prayer,
my family fled both east and west,
my cottage garden seedless now,
strewn 'round with arid grass
like long-abandoned spears,
my children, my flesh and bone,
struggling to walk the middle way.

And I, alone, a thousand miles apart,
imagine my soul to fly like the wild goose,
my heart bereft of home
these nine full autumns.
Like my kin, I watch the now-bright moon
as tears stream down my face —
tonight, five hearts in five far-distant towns
joined in but one desire.

流浪者

A WANDERER'S MORNING SONG
(after Du Shenyan)

A perpetual pilgrim by trade
knows the thrill of the new —
a rising sun through clouds at dawn
drenching the sea with red,
plum blossom and willow, white and lush,
lining the river's banks,
the goldfinch hurried in by spring,
green apples coming on with a flourish.
Suddenly I hear an ancient song —
my heart longs for my home
and I must dry my tears.

明天

THOUGHTS ON NEW YEAR'S EVE
(after Cui Tu)

Long ago I passed the place
where the three roads meet.
On my trek of ten thousand miles
I've dodged avalanche and assassin.
Tonight, forlorn, I walk
through the wild mountain gap
in a country strange,
oppressed by vernal snow.
This servant I love as son, my family far away.
Unmoored, I float through time.
How will I endure tomorrow's
magnificent new year?

THE FINE OLD CYPRESS
(after Du Fu)

In front of the temple, a fine old cypress,
its trunk of burnished copper
and its root of stone.
Rain glides down its thick bark
as its umber leaves touch the sky.
So long its sojourn here,
forty men cannot encircle its girth.
All admire and cherish its rich age.
Clouds besiege it with fronts from Witch Gorge,
as the moon opens its lamp
on the white mountain snow.

Yesterday I climbed the winding path
east to the bright pavilion —
the first lord contrived a hidden palace,
its elegant red door and green lattice
window now bereft —
only deep quiet here, far from town,
among precipitous rocks.
Here a tree can thrive,
lonely, tall, withstanding gale winds.

Its soul sustains bright power,
the source of its straight growth.
A leaning tower requires beam support;
ten thousand oxen could not tilt this tree.

A cypress cannot write its history.
Old and exposed, it's prey to those
who would chop it with scissors or axe.
Its bitter heart cannot escape invasion of
cricket and ant,
yet its fragrant leaves once nested the
very phoenix.
Some value trees only through use.
Does the hermit sigh in seclusion?
Again the frost will come;
again the tree will go on.

PERSPECTIVE
(after Zhang Jiuling)

South of the river red tangerines
sprout on green branches through winter.
In the depth of hibernal chill
their nature is to thrive.
Here! Offer this sweet treat to your eminent
guests!

Seasons still come and go predictably
and fate will smile or frown.
The neophyte will always seek a mentor.
Among your peach trees and your plums,
you may neglect to recall the shade
of the tangerine.

TO MY RETIRED FRIEND
(after Li Bai)

You and I, old friend, have plied our trades,
each in our separate lands. Today,
from dusk to dusk,
we reminisce among the candle's rays,
your hair and mine gone white.
Our youth and strength have ebbed,
our mutual friends now ghosts.
We sigh with labored hearts.
Can it be twenty years
since we two said farewell?
Back then you were a bachelor —
today your decorous children
honor you by entertaining me,
inquire of my travels,
chat awhile, then offer a repast —
scurry to bring forth wine, rich broth,
the delicate leek cut down in mist of night,
rare succulents well steamed with syrup sweet.
You toast to me again and yet again.
We take ten goblets,
drunk on wistfulness.

(continued)

Old men, we would forever
hold our youth —
as sunbeams split two mountains
we have trodden each our road
to find our way.

DRINKING ALONE WITH THE MOON
(after Li Bai)

Alone, as the moon begins its descent,
I pour a cup of wine.
Like a single pansy in a pot, lonely,
I pour the wine.
With no friends near,
I raise a congenial toast,
inviting the bright moon to join me.
My shadow, the moon, and I — a joyful trio.
The faltering moon's done imbibing,
and my shadow apes me like a disciple —
I must drink for us all.
I sing a song to lighten
our way along the road —
a song to welcome spring.
The moon keeps its falling course
as I sing a serenade
and dance, forth and back,
my shadow unconfused.
Together we awaken the season;
together we are joyous.

(continued)

We feel the wine's headiness
and collapse, isolate again.
Together, we were content to stay;
separate again, each of us
longs for our home
as distant as the Milky Way.

倒下

AMUSING MYSELF
(after Li Bai)

Communing
with my bottle of wine,
I find darkness has settled in.
Flowers have fallen
from their bushes
to adorn my clothes.
Drunk, I rise.
Reaching for the moon
I slip into the stream.
The birds have gone
and I am alone.

龍河

ON SEEING LI BAI IN A DREAM
(after Du Fu)

When you departed, I wept.
Again and again we who remain
suffer sorrow and sorrows.
A miasma shrouds
the river of no return;
there I cannot seek news of your fate.
Yet here you are in a dream—
in my mind, your countenance clear!
What net can snag
a feather from your wing?
You pass a distant road
unafraid, your soul at peace.
You come to me through the deep green
maple woods; you disappear
slipping through the narrow
mountain pass at night.
All that's left is the moon
filling my house to the rafters.
Still I wonder where it is you wander.
The river is wide and deep,
the current strong.
If your crossing faltered,
were you prey to the king
of water monsters?

流放

SEEING THE EXILED LI BAI IN A DREAM II
(after Du Fu)

All day the clouds have scudded through the sky;
at midnight, still unsettled, on they stray.
For three nights in a row I've dreamed of you —
my longing brings you right before my eyes.
Although you're in a hurry to depart,
you tell me of the perils of your road:
the storms that vexed the rivers and the lake,
your boat that floundered and your fears that
raged.
You turn and pause; you scratch your snow-white
head
as peace enfolds your patient will once more.

Our capital is clogged with men in hats.
Yet there you are, alone, haggard and low.
Those who believe the tao will take us home
have not seen you grow old with fortune ill.
A thousand autumns, ten thousand years of fame,
are nothing to the man who dies alone.

EAST OF TOWN
(after Wei Yingwa)

I've been cramped
within my cubicle all year —
what relief to venture beyond the town,
toward the pure light of the rising sun.
Wind through the willows
whooshes a sound of peace;
the tall dark mountain
dwarfs my stressful angst.
As I settle near a thicket
to muse beside the stream,
it is fit to find my self.
Mist wafts a fragrance of healing
as the turtledove echoes her song.
Cheerful in seclusion, alone beats my heart.
Time and again I've obeyed
the call of work —
scheming affairs
that hurry me along.
Oh, to retire here!
To build a sturdy hut,
and like my old friend Tao
live true to my own nature,
genuine, ordinary, apt.

AMONG THE CLIFFS
(after Han Yu)

Up the narrow mountain path
through stony crags, bats flit
in twilight as I reach the temple,
ascending the great hall. Good
to rest upon the steps after the rain
by huge banana fronds and lush geraniums.

The monk tells me of murals, portraits
of our prophet. His torch
illuminates the ancient face
holy and sacred underneath this glow.

He readies my bed and sweeps the matted floor,
sets forth hot soup and new-cooked rice.
This frugal meal deeply satisfies.

The night is still — all insects now are mute —
the clear moon climbs above the mountain top,
peeks through my shuttered door.

At dawn I wander, unsure of my path,
which twists and turns through mist and fallen
snow.

(continued)

Though tired and confused, I make a natural way,
with naked foot in azure streams
through alpenglow and stately giant pines
amid the gusts that roar
and flutter out my robe.

Content, I could grow old here,
shunning city ways. A student,
two or three, would find
an ancient soul
upon his proper path.

A REPLY TO THE YOUNG MAYOR
(after Wang Wei)

Now, in old age, I seek the quiet life,
to free my mind of the ten thousand things,
contained within myself, just here and now.
In leisure I'll wander back into the woods —
winds through the pine will tug at my sash belt.
As moonlight floods the mountain
I shall pluck upon my lute.
What logic guides this life of poverty?
Ah, do you hear the fisher as he sings? —
so deep and rich!

TO A CICADA
(after Li Shangyin)

You cannot sate your hunger
even on the tall grasses of summer,
and you are loath to chirp
in vain to empty ears.
By morning your song's grown weak —
the lone pine hears
but neither heeds nor cares.
I have drifted through life too long —
weeds choke my peaceful garden.
So vexed, I take to heart
your prudent reprimand —
to choose the genuine and simple way.

平靜

READING ZEN SCRIPTURE
WITH A TEACHER AT DAWN
(after Liu Zongyuan)

New-drawn water from the well
to cleanse my morning mouth —
its iciness stings my teeth,
and I tremble.
I clear my mind like
brushing dust from my robe,
grasp my treasured text,
and hurry to the eastern room
reading on the way.

These days, one by one,
we neglect our ancient lore.
The truth is deep and hard to understand.
I ripen in study and knowledge
and pray to find my path.

This courtyard is now unequivocally still:
moss covers over all the dark bamboo.
As the sun clears away the mist and dew,
green pines are vivid, seeming newly-washed.

Serenity descends. Words fly away--
I smile, untroubled, simply content to be.

59

周期

INSCRIBED ON THE MOUNTAIN
AT THE NORTH INN
(after Song Zhiwen)

When the sun and moon are southerly,
the wild goose returns.
For me to travel home
I follow nature's way.
The sun must rise and fall;
the river only pauses
as the ebb tide turns.
At twilight the miasma
has not yet filled the forest,
and at dawn I glimpse my home
beyond the white plum blossom.

ANCIENT AIR
(after Li Bai)

Climbing this high,
I can cast my gaze
on four seas.
How vast seems heaven,
vast the earth beneath.
Frost blankets
the crowded plains
of autumn as a cold wind
sweeps the imposing desert.
Along the river flowing east,
magnificence —
the ten thousand things all billow!
Endless clouds float over the sun,
eclipsing its white brilliance.
The parasol tree is alive
with nests of swallows and sparrows,
the phoenix perched
on the thorny jujube.
In time all I see
ripens, ebbs, leaves, and returns.
So do I, sword in hand,
go, singing of the arduous way.

RETURNING HOME
(after He Zhizhang)

As a young boy, I left my town;
now, an oldster, I circle home.
The place seems as it was;
yet I have changed,
my mane of hair
now but a shabby pelt.
Here comes a grandson,
image of myself.
He smiles politely and inquires,
Stranger, where is your home?

KEY TO CHINESE CHARACTERS

Page	Meaning	Characters
1	Independent	独立
2	Arduous road	道
6	Gown	長袍
7	Curtain	帘
8	Rain	防雨
9	Shadow	影
10	Wet tears	眼泪湿
11	Woman's face	女人的脸
12	Jade flute	玉笛
13	Mental suffering	精神痛苦
15	Sadness	悲

"From moon-shadowed loneliness to wine-soaked friendship, from dreary winter rain to spring orchard joy, these elegant homages by Alexandra Mason bring us closer to the nature, people and philosophy of T'ang dynasty China. Reading these poems has me longing again for the ever-unfolding East."
--Henry Hughes, author of "Shutter Lines"

"This selection of poems 'after' ones by T'ang dynasty masters joins a long conversation of poets seeking to bring into their own times what has resonated for them in works from seventh- and eighth-century China. In these versions by Alexandra Mason, we hear the yearning of the exile and of the one left behind; we see the natural world, sometimes as a mirror of personal grief, sometimes as a comfort for it; we feel the struggle to find a true way and to continue on it."
--Eleanor Berry, author of "Green November"

"With a verse for each week of the year, *Poems Along the Way* equips English-speaking readers for a journey through 52 classics from the ancient Chinese masters. This Taoist treasure chest frees fleeting flute notes and turtledoves thousands of years old, gives us pause under the 'sturdy huts' of our ancestors, and braves the same mountain summits as the T'ang Dynasty's finest poets. A very old muse moves through these poems, which guide the student toward enduring truths."
--Matt Schumacher, author of "The Fire Diaries"

Made in the USA
Lexington, KY
08 August 2017